STOP
Blending In

The 7 Steps For Achieving
Thought-Leader Status And
Standing Out In Your Field

ANGELA POINTON

Writing & Publishing Process by
PlugAndPlayPublishing.com

Book Cover by Tracey Miller
TraceOfStyle.com

Edited by Jenny Butterfield

ISBN: 9781695470064

This book is dedicated to all the "blenders" out there who are mustering up the guts to stand out.

Table of Contents

Read This First

Y ou've picked up this book because you realize the importance of establishing your own personal brand.

You know that being seen as a thought leader differentiates you as a businessperson. You know that being an expert allows you to command higher fees for your goods or services.

And you know that being an authority elevates your business and allows you to grab more market share.

But the question is ...

Do You Consider Yourself an Authority?

Most business owners and executives I work with have a hard time with that question. They are confident in their own abilities and skills. They even have a hunch that they could be thought leaders in their fields. But I've discovered that most business owners and executives are modest, and to be seen as an authority is outside of their comfort zone.

Yes, some business owners and executives are egotists and find joy in pounding their chests. This book is not for that kind of executive. This book is also not for the business owner or executive that wants to achieve thought-leader status just because they want fans, notoriety, or for others to bow down to them.

Writing a book for people like that isn't in my DNA. In fact, I relate most to the business owners and executives who are unassuming and skeptical of their own authority. You see, it took me years of people telling me "Wow, you've got something special" or "Gee, you look

at marketing differently" for me to begin realizing I could establish myself as a thought
leader on a topic. And the idea that I could be
an authority did feel a bit uncomfortable at
first.

Perhaps this is true for you, too.

What I've realized in the meantime is most
business owners and executives have an area
of expertise (in business or in life) that they
take for granted. But their area of expertise is
often the very thing that causes people to seek
them out. If you're like me and most of the
business owners or executives I work with,
then your area of expertise is likely at the root
of your authority platform, too.

What Does Being A Thought Leader Get Me, Anyway?

Some people describe this concept as having a
personal brand, being an authority, a subject-
matter expert, or a thought leader. Essentially
all these terms mean the same thing: you're

recognized as *the go-to person,* and you have influence in your market or niche as a result.

There are three, main benefits of focusing on your personal brand:

1. **Growing your revenue and widening your net via referrals.** As people remember you as a thought leader in X or the person that's great at Y, you'll become more memorable to prospects and gain more referrals.

2. **Closing deals faster**. When you're the authority on something, people automatically gain trust in you and feel like they're working with the best. The element of trust is critical in sales, and achieving thought-leader status validates you as someone who knows her or his stuff.

3. **Beating the competition in the game**. By not playing this game, you open the door for your competition to position themselves as the go-to person or company in your field and take customers and clients

away from you. Beat them to it. There's a lot of value for you as the first person that's seen as a thought leader in your field.

Put an End to Being Quiet, Just Because Others are Loud

I wrote this book not to start something but rather to end something. The quieter, less boisterous businesspeople like you and me run the risk of getting stomped on and silenced by the loud, egotistical types. Yet, what I've found time and time again is that the smarts and know-how often resides with the quieter bunch. Inside this book, I've laid out a simple, seven-step process for you to claim your authority and thought-leadership status that puts an end to the way most people do "authority positioning": by being loud, by over-promising, and by using look-at-me marketing.

We'll explore a simpler, more genuine approach in this book. First, we're going to look at what your authority is and how you can leverage your authority (or the authority of someone on your team) to grow your company. Next, you'll learn how to assess your body of work and establish your authority platform. And finally, you'll understand what you need to market your personal brand and achieve thought-leader status, so you can command higher fees and grow your company to new heights.

By the end of this book, you'll appreciate your unique talents and skills, and you'll have a much clearer grasp on the authority you are known for in this world. In addition, you'll feel comfortable telling others that you are the authority and have the confidence to leverage your new thought-leadership status – not to fill your ego but to fill your bank account.

Let's begin.

Chapter 1
Discovering My Authority

I've always considered myself a "blender." That's my made-up word for the kind of person who simply wants to blend in and go unnoticed. But however hard I tried, blending in was difficult for me. Ever since I was a kid, I've had flaming red hair with tangles of curly, wiry locks that refused to adhere to any style other than how they naturally formed: poofy.

For a blender, having flaming red hair was a nightmare! When all I wanted to do is blur into the background, having red hair made disappearing impossible. Every mother, every grandmother, every aunt, checkout clerk, garbage man, and every single passerby stopped to comment on my hair.

Each nightfall, I'd lay my head down on my pillow with the willingness to trade a lifetime of wishes for the ability to transform my hair into straight, boring, mousey brown hair like other girls had.

But instead, I woke up with the same head of hair. Every. Morning.

My desperation to magically acquire boring hair went from severe to off-the-charts on May 21, 1982 when the blockbuster hit movie *Annie* was released.

The world fell in love with this flick, not only because of its fairy-tale story of an orphan that landed in a rich man's mansion, but also because of the adorable, little actress's "unique" short, red, curly hair.

Overnight, the entire population of Central New Jersey stopped commenting on my hair and instead, started grabbing me on my tiny, little six-year-old shoulder. They'd gasp and proceed to shout, "Oh look! It's a real life orphan Annie!" Inevitably they'd then shriek, "the sun'll come out … TOMORROW!"

While most extraverted girls would have felt like they hit the lottery on May 21st, to me, being Annie's doppelganger felt as if the hair gods had played the meanest trick possible.

To hide from the world, I dove into books where I had the ability to stand side-by-side with a character but never be noticed nor actually be part of the story. I even bought issues of **Seventeen Magazine** (years before I was seventeen) and spent hours ripping out tutorials on hair, clothing, and trends — looking for ways to blend into the crowd.

As the years went on, the fanatical **Annie** fans calmed their singing voices. The hair-straightening chemicals and hair rollers that I begged my mom to use worked an acceptable level of magic, resisting what my hair naturally wanted to do. Finally, seventeen years, four months, and fifteen days after *Annie* was released, my red hair became my advantage. On this day, my husband-to-be (although I didn't know it at the time) walked up to me on a cold Philadelphia sidewalk and introduced himself by saying, "Hi, my name is Jesse. I really like your hair." On that day, I finally learned standing out isn't such a bad thing after all.

Not until many years later, when I told this story to a group of entrepreneurs, did I realize this story held a critical lesson: if you're going to become an authority in your field, you will have to embrace your uniqueness and follow the steps necessary to stop blending in.

Yes, this story is silly, detailing my woes and my red hair. But the truth is that virtually everyone desired that red hair in the early 80's. Instead of acknowledging my unique advantage and embracing that what I had was special, I tried to bury that specialness.

Consciously or unconsciously, I see many entrepreneurs and business folks doing the same thing. But the most important people to you and your business appreciate you for how you stand out. They choose you because of your specialness. And they stay with you because of it too. So, if you want more people to utilize your business and appreciate your authority and your uniqueness, you have to tell more people that you're different and show them how you're unique.

Learning to Stand Out Can Be Challenging, Especially for a Blender

After graduating from grad school and beginning a career in marketing, I fell in love with entrepreneurial business and went on to spend the majority of my career helping entrepreneurs market their products and services. After assisting dozens of entrepreneurs in their marketing efforts, I began to notice two things.

First, the businesses that would sit back and wait for sales leads to come in often struggled.

But the businesses that would go out and do live speaking engagements to their target markets about their industry or their work would often succeed. In fact, when I compared similar businesses, the business that was run by a CEO who made a point to establish him or herself as an authority was hands-down always more successful than the businesses run by a CEO who didn't.

Now, I know what you're thinking. You're thinking, "That makes sense because the CEO probably came back from a speaking engagement with a handful of business opportunities." And you're correct. That CEO would come back with more business opportunities.

However, what you may not realize is that the businesses that sent a leader out to speak also had an increase in their other marketing efforts too. Their websites performed better, their email lists were bigger, and their social media platforms got more engagement.

You might also be thinking, "Wait a second, I didn't realize this would be a book about speaking." It's not. This example simply demonstrates that the mere act of putting oneself in a position of authority generates immediate, ongoing, cascading, and positive impact to a business.

For every one of my clients that had a team member that regularly spoke to audiences, there were at least nine other clients that didn't. So, like any good marketer that witnesses positive results, I wanted to share these findings with others. I began encouraging clients to start with something small: approach another website and submit a guest blog post or ask an industry association to be a guest on their podcast.

And that's when I noticed the second thing: not everyone likes to stand out and be the center of attention. Just as the case was for me in the early 80's, some people enjoy blending in. And for those CEOs who were used to blending in, you'd be surprised how difficult it was for them to even take a small step toward standing out.

I'll never forget the day one of my clients agreed to do a webinar for a publication in his field, which was related to compensation and human resources. On the day of the webinar, I joined in to listen to my client's presentation. He showed up and introduced himself, and the webinar ended there. He couldn't proceed out of fear and simply disconnected himself from the webinar, leaving the editor of the publication and the audience hanging in silence.

Being in a position of authority made him freeze, clam up, and bolt out of the spotlight as fast as he could.

He's certainly not alone. Fear stops most people from peeking their heads out of the crowd and being heard or seen.

I can relate. At my very first job after college, my boss asked me to participate on a webinar and present five slides from the comfort of my desk. Before show time, I spent the entire morning in the bathroom with a sour stomach. Eventually, I got myself together in time to make the event and stuck with my presentation for the duration. Afterward, I felt great and very proud of myself. But I also felt a bit embarrassed at how upset I let myself get about something that turned out to be relatively easy.

When you're used to blending in, even the early stages of establishing authority can be challenging. But I assure you. If you stick with your commitment to start standing out, you'll become more and more comfortable with the tasks involved in building one's authority.

Discovering Your Authority

Whether you feel more comfortable in the spotlight or behind the scenes, I want to encourage you to take the necessary actions to position yourself as an authority in the marketplace — whether you're the CEO or a key employee. Why?

Because, like I said, businesses that have thought leaders inside of them succeed more often than the businesses that don't. Authority businesses don't have to shout louder than their competition by spending big dollars on ad campaigns. Authority businesses don't have to market just as heavy as their competition by being at every trade show, sponsorship opportunity, and print magazine. People are magnetically attracted to authority businesses. Clients look forward to hearing from authority businesses so much so that they proactively seek out the authorities and leaders.

So, how do you discover your authority and establish yourself as a thought leader in the marketplace? There are three possible methods for discovering your authority that we'll discuss briefly here.

The first path is listening to what your partners and customers are telling you makes you unique. For example, my personal journey to discovering my own authority began when my clients pointed out that my approach was different from the other marketing consultants they had dealt with in the past. While other marketing consultants were strictly talking about traditional marketing avenues, I would ask questions like, "So tell me the last time you spoke to an audience of prospects?" Or, "Have you ever thought of being a guest on an industry podcast?" Or even, "Shouldn't you start a podcast of your own on this topic?"

Through client feedback, I discovered that I had a knack for pushing entrepreneurs to get out of their comfort zones and start doing little things, one at a time, to build their authority. For my clients brave enough to venture down a path toward building authority, our relationship became unique and stronger than I had ever imagined.

Admittedly, I took a year or two to notice this difference. But once I listened to what clients were saying about what made me unique, I began to capitalize on my process and started to build my own authority. Now, I'm seen as a thought leader in helping people like you elevate their own authority and establish their companies as market leaders. I've become the authority on authority.

When you start consciously listening to your clients and partners through regular conversation, feedback surveys, Google reviews, and more, you'll begin to notice commonalities on where the potential resides for defining and building your authority.

The second path to discovering your own authority is when you listen to the marketplace and leverage a change in the market to establish yourself as the thought leader on that specific change. For example, there might be a new technology on the horizon related to your business or a new way of doing something because of a change in laws. When this opportunity happens, authority often establishes itself based on whichever company or person leverages a change in the market first.

The third and final path comes down to legacy. Instead of your authority being born out of your business, your authority is based on *the thing* for which you want to be known and remembered.

The teachings in this book are relevant to all three paths and will be explored in the chapters to come. And the majority of what I'll share in this book is intended to provide an easy, how-to guide for those that naturally feel uncomfortable being seen as an authority. But before we get to that, let's explore a concept I call, "The Authority Multiplier" and which person at your business should be known as the authority.

Chapter 2
The Authority Multiplier

M any people often assume that the CEO of a company should be the authority at that organization. CEOs are usually the ones with the vision. And most times, they're the ones with the most passion about the overall business strategy. They're also the head honchos and the one people naturally look toward for leadership.

However, I'd like to suggest another strategy that is rarely considered. I call this strategy the "Authority Multiplier," and it has the ability to leapfrog you over your competition and help you dominate your marketplace in short order.

How does the Authority Multiplier work? With a simple equation: the number of Authorities multiplied by the number of Areas of Expertise = Your Authority Multiplier.

Here's how the strategy works. Let's say a business only leverages the CEO as a thought leader and authority. That business's Authority Multiplier equals one (one authority x one area of expertise). However, when a business is comprised of multiple thought leaders and authority platforms, all specializing in one area of expertise, that same company's Authority Multiplier skyrockets.

Let's take a look at an example to really understand how this works. There are roughly one hundred lawyers inside the Philadelphia office of Fox Rothschild, a large legal firm with multiple locations across the country. Each lawyer concentrates on a different legal niche. One lawyer might specialize in wealth planning, another lawyer in franchised businesses, another lawyer in human resources, and so on.

So, if Fox Rothschild's Philly office has 100 thought leaders exclusively focusing on a unique area of law, then their Authority Multiplier equals 100 (100 authorities x one area of expertise for each person). Because of this, their Authority Multiplier is 100 times more powerful than a competing law office leveraging only the CEO as the single authority at the firm.

Look around, and you'll quickly realize that leveraging the Authority Multiplier is pretty darn rare. For most companies, if anyone is seen as an authority, it's the big kahuna and no one else. We could examine why this is, but that might make for a whole other book on leadership psyche and ego. What's more important to understand is the big opportunity that other companies' deficiencies create for you!

Are you wondering what sort of activities individual employees of your organization might take on to build your company's Authority Multiplier?

In Fox Rothschild's case, what if the lawyer specializing in franchise law simply organized a quarterly panel discussion with some local, franchise-industry thought leaders? The panel might consist of a few local franchisors, a franchise marketing firm, and perhaps a person from a franchise lending institution. If all the panel participants, plus a member of the Fox Rothschild team, co-marketed the event, the panel would have a high likelihood of drawing in potential clients for Fox Rothschild's franchise law division. Plus, the lawyer at Fox Rothschild who organized the event would quickly become known as one of the top franchise lawyers in the Philadelphia region, especially after running such an event routinely.

Now, envision that entire, nation-wide organization of Fox Rothschild's 900 lawyers were executing quarterly events like the one I just described. You can quickly see how prolific and varied the authority of one company can become when multiple thought leaders are leveraged.

Shout Out to All the Employees Reading This

If you're an employee of an organization and you're reading this book, I want to give you a major shout out. You're more than an employee. You're most likely an intrapreneur, which is an employee working within a larger organization who acts like a product innovator or entrepreneur. As an intrapreneur, you're inventive and creative, and you likely already see the benefits of leveraging your authority on behalf of the organization or the benefit of your own career. The contents and advice within this book are easily adaptable to help you, and the sky's the limit for your career if you implement these techniques.

In just a moment, we'll explore how you can find authorities in your organization and increase your own Authority Multiplier. But first, if you're a solopreneur reading this book, you might be asking, "How am I going to leverage multiple authorities in my business? It's just me!"

This is a valid question that both solopreneurs and CEOs of larger businesses can learn from, so let's take a look at that challenge.

Leverage Your Vendors' and Partners' Authority Assets (Even if You're a Solopreneur)

Do you outsource certain parts of your operations to others, or do you bring on companies you partner with? If you do, then you can use the Authority Multiplier by leveraging the authority of your vendors and companies with which you partner.

You see, your vendors and partners are, in essence, part of your team. So, the strength of their authority has the potential to increase your business' authority as well.

For example, let's say you're a master chef with a portfolio of restaurants, and all of your vegetables are sourced from local farmers. If those local farmers ran events where they spoke or gave demos of their produce in your dishes, wouldn't the authority of those farmers boost your restaurant's own brand? Of course it would!

But that's just the tip of the iceberg. You could partner up and co-promote these events on your websites, to your email lists, and on your social media accounts. And they could do the same. You and your farmers could also leverage one another's networks to encourage others to share the event, create strategically placed flyers, and so much more. Do you see the power in partnering up and leveraging each other's authority?

Now, what if you're a solopreneur who owns a professional services business? Can you use this strategy? Of course you can. Let's say you're an independent financial advisor specializing in helping baby boomers save for retirement. What if you partnered with an estate attorney who also focuses on helping baby boomers and boomer children?

You could leverage your relationship and collaborate on a webinar or an in-person event. The estate attorney would speak about estate planning for boomers, and you would speak about protecting the boomer's wealth.

Similar to the example above, co-marketing the event doubles the amount of people you'd otherwise invite if you were the only one in charge of hosting and inviting.

Whether you run a big business or you're a solopreneur, you should now see how you can use the Authority Multiplier strategy with vendors and partners.

Recruiting Stronger Partners And Vendors

No matter which industry you're in or which type of business you own, if you're going to use the Authority Multiplier strategy, you may want to consider your partners and vendors using a new set of criteria. Ask your potential partners about their willingness to co-market together and to leverage their authority with your authority. If they say 'no,' they might still make a great partner, but they won't elevate your Authority Multiplier. Continue your search to see if there's an equally good partner out there that will!

How to Start Using the Authority Multiplier Strategy

Now that you understand the power behind the Authority Multiplier strategy, let's talk about how you can start using this strategy to grow your reach and your profits.

The first step to using the Authority Multiplier strategy is to identify an employee who you can see as a thought leader inside your company. Or identify a vendor or partner you can see joining forces with to leverage one another's authority.

After reading the first few pages of this chapter, you probably already have someone in mind. However, I want to caution you to read the next paragraph before you run out and tell anyone your plan. Why? Because the most important step in this process is asking the individual for their willingness to participate.

Some people just aren't ready to be thought leaders. And that's okay. Communicating with your employee, vendor, or partner is imperative, and identifying if he or she is a good fit for this strategy is just as important. Otherwise, you'll waste your time and energy trying to elevate his or her authority, only to meet resistance every step of the way.

So, I recommend you start by having a conversation with the individuals you have in mind, and determine their readiness to participate in a strategic, authority venture together.

For vendors and partners, I suggest setting up a meeting and having a conversation about the advantages your partnership will have for their company. If you approach someone running another business and ask for her help solely because the venture will benefit your business, your request will fall on deaf ears. Instead, prepare for the conversation by creating a list of the ways in which this will help the other business. Present the opportunity by highlighting those ways, and you'll find that you'll get greater buy-in. Additionally, your partners will likely approach the opportunity with much more enthusiasm if they can visualize everything that they'll potentially gain from participating.

Some of the ways partners would benefit might be:

- Exposure to your audience

- More visibility to prospective customers

- Elevating their own authority

- More traffic to their website

- Growing their email list

- Exposure to the media

The same concept applies to when approaching employees. You must think through the ways this strategy benefits them (not just you and your company), and make sure you have a few advantages noted.

These are the most common benefits for the employee(s) participating:

- Escalating career advancement

- Adding to their resume

- Establishing their own influence within the industry or their field

- Demonstrating leadership and initiative

- Experience, stretching their abilities, and personal growth

Sit down with your employee, and discuss his or her interest level in speaking, writing, or being interviewed on behalf of the organization. Explain all the ways these efforts will improve their career and position at the organization.

Lastly, when approaching any employee, vendor, or partner, please keep in mind the story I told you about in Chapter One where one of my clients agreed to do a webinar but hung up after introducing himself. His fear took over, and he shut down. You might find that once you try elevating the authority of others, some people simply don't have the comfort level required to participate. Some people are just not cut out for this work, or they're just not ready yet. And that's okay. Don't force anyone into speaking or even writing on behalf of your organization unless he or she feels comfortable moving forward, and you feel confident that they're comfortable.

A wonderful, low-risk method for trying out someone's comfort level and eagerness to participate is asking an employee, vendor, or partner to write a blog post for your company's own website. Agree to give an author credit and a bio at the end of the blog.

For a partner, also include a link to his or her website within the bio. These things will help them see the value in participating.

For you, a blog post provides a low-risk opportunity to evaluate how enthusiastic they are about participating, their ability to follow through, as well as the quality of their thought-leadership efforts.

What If You Don't Have Any Thought Leaders Around You?

Like I mentioned in the last section, when most people learn about this strategy, they immediately start thinking about employees in their company they can elevate and leverage or vendors and partners they can pursue. However, what if no one is popping into your mind?

The ugly truth is that you may not be comfortable with the thought leadership of your employees, vendors, or partners. If this is the case, here are three potential reasons why this might be.

First, you might not feel that your employees have a particular strength in one area. This issue speaks to a slightly different root problem, however. If you are passionate about building the influence and presence of your company, then you must align yourself with employees, vendors, and partners that are thought leaders. When hiring, look for candidates that bring subject matter expertise to the table. This doesn't mean that every, single employee you bring on has to be someone qualified as a thought leader. But thought leadership should be a decision-making point during the hiring process for key, strategic positions at the company. The same is true when you're bringing on vendors and partners. Look for potential vendors and partners who are already established experts in their fields. Doing so will increase your ability to use the Authority Multiplier strategy.

Second, you may be uncomfortable with allowing individuals other than yourself to represent your company because you're afraid they'll say something false, embarrassing, or make a mistake. Just like the first reason, this requires more digging. Giving up on building your company's authority because you're worried an employee, vendor, or partner will mess up is silly. We're human, so making a mistake is inevitable. However, if you can help your people outline ways in which they'll participate in sharing their thought leadership, you may be able to alleviate the risks and ease your mind.

Last, you might struggle with the idea of elevating the thought leadership of an employee because of the risk that this thought-leader employee might leave your organization. Or, in the case of a business partner, you may worry about whether or not the partnership will come to an end down the road. In most cases, elevating an employee's exposure and asking him or her to represent the company in this way is going to serve as a retention mechanism. As for partners or vendors, relationships do end sometimes. Forgoing the maximization of those relationships while they do exist is shortsighted, however.

Yes, all of the above are fair reservations. Allowing someone else other than you to step into the spotlight can be a scary proposition. However, if you're still uncomfortable leveraging multiple authorities, consider this: if you don't establish your company as an authority in the market by nominating and leveraging multiple thought leaders both inside and outside your organization, one of your competitors surely will. Wouldn't you rather your organization be established as the market leader versus a competitor?

If you answered 'yes,' then I encourage you to think through this strategy – as well as the deeper issues you may be experiencing – and figure out how you can best use the Authority Multiplier strategy to grow your business.

Looking to just dip your toe in and try out thought leadership for yourself, first? I applaud you. Simply trying is more than most people do, and I'm certain that the gains you'll receive will encourage you to do even more in the future.

Now that you understand the Authority Multiplier strategy and how multiple authorities can be leveraged – whether you're a CEO, entrepreneur, solopreneur, or intrapreneur – let's dive deeper into a step-by-step plan for how you can solidify yourself as an authority.

Chapter 3

Step 1: Assess Your Body of Work

"Why should anyone believe I'm the authority on this topic?" It's an important question to ponder. And it's probably the question that's held thousands of people back from claiming thought-leader status on their respective areas of expertise.

People often wonder if they have enough marketable assets, proof points, and track record to secure the reputation they're seeking. The secret truth we'll dissect in this chapter is that you don't have to wait until a comprehensive inventory of proof points is built before telling the world you're the authority.

The Critical Moment Of Deciding To Become "It"

As Pamela Slim, author of ***Body of Work,*** explained in her 2014 TEDx Talk, "Your body of work becomes your brand, your purpose, and your personal legacy." But I'm going to suggest a slight change to what my friend, Pam, stated. And that's the idea that your body of work doesn't *become* those things when it's done. Your body of work forms your purpose and legacy the moment you start.

Meaning, the moment you decide to build a reputation and claim thought-leader status for a particular topic area, you've taken the most critical step.

That's because this step causes you to view your actions differently. It'll make you pause before making certain decisions. It also may cause you to go after bigger opportunities or alliances that once seemed out of your league. And you'll start marketing in a way that you otherwise wouldn't, as we'll explore in future chapters.

Once you begin making decisions about which people or companies you tether yourself to, how you elevate your reputation, and what you want the world to see you as the authority in, you've taken the biggest strategic marketing step any one individual or organization can take.

You may feel like you're faking your authority in the beginning, and that's okay. Feeling uncomfortable in this new skin is normal.

Take one of my own past authority marketing endeavors as an example. I graduated with a Bachelor's Degree in Photography, but after graduating, I never picked up a camera or got paid to shoot images. Even though I had the degree, I was never really a photographer. Instead, I went right back to school for my M.B.A. and started my career in marketing.

But, I always dreamt of marrying my two interests.

One day, while doing something as mundane as painting a room in our new house, I thought about quitting my day-job at the marketing agency I worked at. I wanted to become *the authority* on marketing a photography business. And so a few months later, I quit my job and did just that.

Sure, I had degrees in both topics. But I never owned a photography business, and I didn't have a lengthy resume for marketing photography businesses. Those were two valid excuses that I could have used as to why I shouldn't try to achieve thought-leader status in marketing photography businesses. And believe me – there were many more! Other marketers were already in that space and who was I to say – as the newbie in the field – that I was better?

Alas, I forged ahead and set up a website, started blogging, and cultivated relationships with some of the biggest authorities in the industry. I'll come back to this example a little later in this book to tell you how I landed a magazine columnist position for the largest photography organization in America and how I secured paid keynotes at photography conferences. But for now just know that once you decide to become "it," you're becoming it.

No Proof Points? No Problem.

What if you've never thought to collect proof points before? What if your body of work is all over the place? Or what if you feel like you have nothing to show for your expertise at all?

Don't worry! I've got you covered. In fact, I find that most people don't recognize their authority as well as the potential of other authorities within their companies. Yet oftentimes, the authority is there – lying dormant – waiting to be discovered and leveraged. And that's because they've been building a body of work, or proof points, without realizing the accumulation that's occurred.

For others, they've built multiple bodies of work that are disjointed. They might be experts in one area that is totally disconnected or distinct from another area in which they also excel. Entrepreneurs and intrapreneurs are often fascinated and motivated to build new things, and as a result, experience can be vast and varied.

And yet others have a dream of being the authority in something of which they have minimal proof points. They're more like me when I decided to quit my career and make a hard turn in another direction.

All three scenarios are acceptable. No matter which category you currently fit into, building your authority can begin at any stage. Remember, you have to begin somewhere.

How To Begin Collecting Proof Points

A body of work will grow at an equal rate to which you collect experience and proof points. The more you do, the more you collect, and the more you collect, the more your body of work expands. And most importantly, proving you're a thought leader becomes easier.

In the case of starting from scratch with no proof points, there are two scenarios you can use to start gathering proof points right away. One is gaining an education, certification, or other training to help you know more about your topic of interest. The other is in volunteering free services in exchange for a testimonial from a client, case study, or other tangible validation of your work. You may be able to charge for your services or provide a special "beta rate" to some trial customers. But either way, you don't have to work for free or at a discounted rate for long. Just gain a couple of proof points, and you'll be on your way to charging the right price for this same work.

If you've already built up a few proof points and feel you have foundational training on your topic, then you can leapfrog past the above-mentioned activities. Instead, you want to begin inventorying your body of work to assess all the assets at your disposal for beginning with as strong of an authority platform as possible.

The assets you might inventory include:

- Customer testimonials

- Case studies

- Client logos from well-known entities

- Past speaking engagements

- Videos you've done on the topic

- Articles or write-ups you've been included in

- Awards you've won

Don't worry if you don't have many of these things (yet!). As I've mentioned many times, beginning is more impactful than a killer body of work from the start. Validation by the way of proof points is nice to have, but a rock-solid body of work is rarely where people start.

In Chapter Six, we'll outline how to use these proof points in the first piece of marketing you'll build: your new website. But before we do that, let's dive into your authority topic of choice and make sure you're seriously clear on that first.

Since you're reading this book, you likely have a hunch about what you want to be known for. This hunch might be muddy, vague, or clouded up by too many ideas and that's okay. In the next chapter, I'll help you clarify your vision for your authority, make your vision succinct, and define your vision so it's memorable.

Chapter 4

Step 2: Establish Your Authority Platform

I believe that brand loyalty is almost extinct. We're all witnessing the end of a marketing advantage that so many companies and entrepreneurs once enjoyed. With plentiful options and numerous methods with which to buy, coupled with lower-than-ever barriers to commercial entry, consumers are more in control than ever before, because there are simply more companies and more choices.

Now, don't get all caught up in the doom and gloom of brand loyalty disappearing. Because of this economic movement, companies and individual professionals need to get clearer on their competitive advantages. And just by reading this book and starting to position yourself as a thought leader, you're adopting one of the easiest ways to establish your competitive advantage.

Truthfully, creating a personal brand and building one's authority is a rare, untapped opportunity for the majority of businesses and professionals. But personal branding, or the ongoing process of establishing a prescribed image or impression in the minds of others, can help you establish the competitive advantage you're looking for.

However, your authority platform and your personal brand can only be your competitive advantage if two things are clear to both you and the people you target. First, you must define your authority platform in one or two clear and specific sentences. Second, you must define your audience and what you'll be known for to that audience.

What's The One Thing You Want To Be Known For?

This is a simple question, but it's so difficult to answer. Humans are complex, careers are varied, and innovative, smart people tend to be multi-faceted. In other words, picking one super-clear direction is not easy.

I often find that the reason why people get foggy and confused when trying to answer this question is either because the individual has a lack of clarity or because he or she hasn't gotten specific enough. Let me give you two examples.

The first example is Gary Smith, an entrepreneur who started two businesses from scratch. One was a smoothie company that shipped vitamin-laced beverage mixes to workout fanatics' doorsteps each week. His other business was a non-profit organization aimed at helping Fortune 500 corporations create better experiences for their college interns. Gary wanted to be known for both. He wanted to be the healthy smoothie guru, and he also wanted to be known for creating the pathway from internships to bright careers for college students.

Those two authority topics couldn't be more different. Different thought leadership, different audiences, and different platforms.

If you're like Gary and you have numerous topics you're a thought leader in, consider these questions:

- Which topic do you have the largest body of work in or have the most passion for further expanding your body of work in?

- Which topic connects you with your best customers or career trajectory?

- Which topic excites you the most?

Gary's topics are too varied to be combined into a single, authority platform. Could he have two? Maybe. But most people I meet don't have the time or the capital to do the marketing to build an authority for more than one business. My advice to virtually everyone is to pick one direction based on the answers to the questions above.

Now, while Gary Smith was too varied in his topics, let's explore Sara Brown's situation next. Sara has a problem with lack of specificity. Sara is a life coach and wants to be known as a "rock star" coach. I probed her with questions such as, "Tell me what you mean by that?" She responded by saying, "That's it. I just want to be known as being the best coach, the one with the best sessions, and the best customer service. I want to be a rock star coach."

Sara's authority platform is simply not specific enough. And that's because – without doing any research – I know that 100% of life coaches also want to be known as the best. Can you imagine a segment of life coaches that want to be mediocre or known as the worst at what they do? It's not likely. In just about any market, being known as a rock star or the best is too common to be a legitimate authority platform.

If you're like Sara and you're having trouble getting clear and specific about your authority platform, consider these questions:

- What area or niche within your area of expertise are you most passionate about?

- Is how you do what you do or the process you take people through unique in any way?

- Is your knowledge or desired outcome something that's special or different?

Getting clear on your topic and specific on how you're unique is vital to your success and establishing your authority.

Take me, for example. I took years to get clear and specific. So, how do I define my authority and personal brand?

"I help professionals become thought leaders, and I help companies elevate their authority so they can earn more money."

Who I help is clear: professionals and companies.

What I do is clear: create thought leaders and elevate a company's authority platform.

The desired outcome is clear: earning more money.

Do I have a body of work that's full of proof points? Yes.

Am I interested in further educating myself in this area and building a bigger body of work? Absolutely.

Another great question to consider is, can I earn more money if I utilize my topic as my authority platform? The answer for me is 'yes.' If you're uncertain about the ways in which your authority platform might boost revenue, don't worry. We'll explore the revenue potential of your authority platform in the next chapter.

Whether you're like Gary or more like Sara, know that authority platforms aren't built overnight. Clarity and specificity rarely dawn upon people without spending time answering the questions mentioned in this chapter. Take more time to dive deeper into these questions by researching other authorities in your areas of interest or by asking your customers what they like best about you.

Once you have an idea for your authority platform, the next step is making sure you know the kinds of people that will love learning all about what you're teaching. These people are your "tribe." They're the individuals that'll likely get huge grins on their faces when they learn you're the authority on something they care about. And this enthusiasm happens because the people that make up your tribe have been secretly waiting and wishing for you.

As Seth Godin, best-selling author of the book *Tribes: Why We Need You To Lead Us* defines this very idea by saying, "A tribe is a group of people connected to one another, connected to a leader, and connected to an idea. For millions of years, human beings have been part of one tribe or another."

Let's envision the people that'll make up your tribe by working on your audience persona.

Develop Your Audience Persona

An audience persona is similar to a customer persona you may have developed at your company. However, your audience persona consists of the people that'll find your intelligence fascinating and are eager to hear more from you. They're your tribe members. Often, the reason they're so interested is because of the desired outcome your authority platform promises.

For example, let's pretend that Gary decided that being a "smoothie guru" was his authority platform. And after working on defining his authority platform a little more, Gary determined that he would be the expert on healthy smoothies for workout fanatics looking to become more energetic and stronger at the gym.

Gary's promised outcome is "becoming more energetic and stronger at the gym." He's going to show his audience how to do that by illustrating what healthy smoothies are best for certain workout goals. When we think about the audience for Gary's authority platform, the persona is pretty clear: workout fanatics.

If your audience is a bit varied, that's okay. For example, Gary's group of workout fanatics might include new moms returning to exercise after giving birth, as well as men that hit the gym five days a week after work. The tolerance for that variety is up to you. If you love working with a variety of people, great! If you prefer to only include specific niches in your audience, that's fine too.

I choose to include many different types of entities in my audience persona. For example, I work with enterprise-level executives at large organizations as well as solopreneurs and entrepreneurs with smaller companies. Additionally, I also work with politicians, advocates, and individuals who have no business other than the business of professional speaking. All these individuals have the same desired outcome, however. They all want to earn more money by achieving thought-leader status.

When crafting an audience persona, be sure to include all of the people that make up that audience. Over time, pay attention to how that audience changes – either when the types of people that love your thought leadership become more specific, or when your audience grows more diverse by including new types of people you didn't originally consider.

As your audience persona becomes clearer to you or changes, revisit the notion that your thought leadership must always deliver your desired outcome. The desired outcome you promise your audience should always be the outcome your audience is most interested in learning about. For example, let's say Gary started attracting seniors to his healthy smoothies. The desired outcome for this audience might not be the same as the average workout fanatic. For seniors, the desired outcome of buying from Gary might be consuming healthier liquids during the day, so they live longer. Should your audience begin to change, your desired outcomes may need to be re-articulated to address new outcomes you're still suited to deliver.

Similarly, if your audience becomes more specific or more niched, your desired outcomes may become more specific, as well, to directly appeal to a tighter group of people. For example, let's say Sara decided to become a life coach for working professionals, but she then started getting hired by more and more people looking to make drastic career changes. The desired outcome of Sara's services might change from helping people who work to helping working people nurture their bravery and navigate the uncertainty that is required when making a drastic career change.

As time moves on, always check to make sure the desired outcomes of your audience persona are aligned by answering this question: is my promised outcome still the outcome my audience persona desires when working with me?

Another reason why keeping an eye on your audience is critical is because the personal brand you create for yourself when building your authority platform needs to be in sync. Let's discuss that topic next.

Creating A Personal Brand

As stated in Chapter Two, as soon as you decide to become an authority on a topic, you've begun. Hopefully, you're starting to tell more and more people about your expertise, even in casual conversation. If you've ever had a conversation with someone that fits your audience persona, you know you're onto something if they ask you, "Where can I find out more?"

If you stare at them blankly without a good response to that question, this section will help you. Your authority platform needs a home. It needs a place where people can learn more.

There are three wonderful places for your authority platform to call home. The first is in a book like the one you're reading, the second is on a company's team bio page or your LinkedIn profile, and the third is on your very own website. Let's explore each, and you'll be able to quickly decide which options are best for you.

Many individuals that get paid to speak or that generate big dollars for their companies write a book. If you've written a book or are thinking of writing a book that is synonymous with your authority platform, use that book. When people ask you, "Where can I find out more?" gift them a copy or tell them where they can buy your book. This tactic will become a large part of your personal branding strategy.

Second, if you're part of a large company with multiple authorities, consider altering the bios on your website's "About" pages to clearly include the authority platforms of each individual on the team. Make sure each person's bio starts with that person's role and what he or she is a thought leader in. Similarly, encouraging individual authorities to share content specific to their thought leadership topic on their individual LinkedIn or other social media profiles is wise. If you're the CEO of the organization, you should be doing this on your profile too.

The third and final common way to brand your authority platform is on your own website. We'll talk about your website in detail in Chapter Six. For now, I want you to realize that individual thought leaders should strongly consider purchasing their name as a domain.

If your name is common, consider including a middle initial, hyphen, or a creative website domain. The website www.DrinksByGary.com

might be easier to obtain than a website using Gary's very common last name of Smith. Although Angela Pointon isn't a very common name at all, there is a ceramist in Europe that bought that domain. Therefore, my website uses a hyphen and is Angela-Pointon.com.

Here's where things get even more exciting. Now that you've begun thinking through how you'll establish your authority platform, you'll be able to clearly see the ways in which you can earn additional money with your platform. In the next chapter, we'll dive into six different ways your authority platform can generate money.

Chapter 5

Step 3: The 6 Obvious Ways to Make Money with Your Authority Platform

The author Russ von Hoelscher once said, "I never cease to be amazed at the huge number of folks who have valuable information between their ears who don't consider packing and selling it." I feel the same way.

If you're interested in not only becoming known as *the person* who is the best at your authority topic, but you also want to earn more money teaching and sharing what you know, this chapter is for you!

In this chapter, we'll touch on six different ways you can earn money with your authority. The goal of this chapter isn't to provide a full tutorial on how to execute on each of the six ideas. There are plenty of authorities out there that are the masters on each topic with oodles of how-to advice!

For now, let's simply review the six ways listed here, and then you'll decide if they're worth exploring further. As we go through each of the common examples of how people earn money, perhaps a few will jump out as possibilities you haven't yet considered.

My suggestion is to start with one way of making money and explore its potential by doing some testing to determine if the strategy you selected will be a revenue generator for you. If, through that testing, you prove that revenue potential exists, work on systematizing the approach to create the most revenue possible.

At that point, move onto testing the next revenue opportunity you find appealing and repeat the process.

1. Write A Book And Sell It

I've spent time studying the reasons why people write non-fiction books. And what I've found is that book authors fall into three general categories.

For some people, the book is burning inside of them. Like a virus, they've got to get their ideas and knowledge out of their system and onto paper. You'll hear people in this category say things like, "It was in me and just had to come out." That's their reason for writing the book. For these people, many don't necessarily think about earning money from the book until after the book is written.

The second reason people write a book is because they want to intentionally earn money from the book. Many successful book authors who fall into this category and earn substantial money from their books already have a following and are considered household names in their industries or niches. Getting a book is like gaining access to the author's brain. And because of this pent-up demand, books in this category earn significant revenue in book sales.

The third and most common reason people write a book is to use the book as a piece of marketing collateral. The book isn't written for any other purpose than to build authority, open doors, and be used as a leave-behind. Before these authors even started writing, they already knew that their books were going to be used to market some other bigger ticket items or services.

While each category is a fine reason to write a book, I'd encourage you to only consider the second and third categories for your own revenue growth purposes. If you're thinking of writing a book, honestly consider whether your book will earn you big dollars. If writing a book likely won't increase your earning power, think about how a book can open doors and create opportunities if you use the book as a marketing tool instead.

2. Paid Keynote Talks

A large portion of the people I serve in my business want to get more paid speaking gigs. Earning $5,000, $10,000, or $20,000 per talk, plus paid travel expenses, can be an attractive revenue stream for many people—especially those that enjoy visiting new places.

For these folks, delivering the talk doesn't feel like work. In fact, many secretly think that getting paid to share their experiences with audiences is kind of absurd, especially knowing that someone else works hard to attract the audience to the event in the first place. Keynote speakers show up, deliver a show-stopping talk, hang out for a bit, and then head home or onto the next gig. All the while, the people in the room give them energy, and they get to see some cool sights between stops.

An added bonus is collecting big, fat checks along the way.

Delivering a keynote talk and commanding large fees is an opportunity for anyone with an authority platform that suits a broad message. On the other hand, if your topic is so instructional and mechanical that your speech must be delivered in a small, intimate setting or with heavy, technical details, a keynote talk might not be right for you. Instead, you might consider a smaller working session that we'll explore next.

3. Workshops

Workshops are great revenue opportunities if your authority platform can teach people how to do something differently, understand a technical topic, or work through a process.

Like paid keynote talks, conducting workshops doesn't necessarily mean you'll have to organize the attendees. You could partner with another organization or industry publication to market the workshop to its members. Your job is to simply show up and deliver the content, and the promoter or organization assembles the audience.

You might decide you want to organize the workshop, host the workshop yourself, and keep all of the revenue. Perhaps you're really talented at event marketing or just cannot think of a group to align yourself with for a workshop.

Event planning is not for the faint of heart, however. If you decide to go this route, make sure to study how events are orchestrated, and plan far out in advance.

Either way, workshops are a great opportunity to gather individuals in a more intimate, collaborative environment where you can teach them something related to your authority platform.

4. Selling Or Licensing Intellectual Property

Marketing your personal brand and building your authority will likely create demand for your time, intelligence, and advice. If you have information that other people need to know, you likely have an opportunity to sell that intellectual property in some form or another.

Selling your intelligence might come in the form of paid hourly consulting. Or perhaps, you'll get paid to teach others a methodology, process, or technique.

For example, you might offer your services in a simple, hourly fee for your time. Or, you might build a training curriculum and charge for completing the program.

As many online content marketers and course creators have proven, building an online educational program and selling that program as an evergreen product online is very possible.

If you're thinking that you don't want to be a coach, educator, or consultant, consider licensing your intellectual property to others instead. In this model, you're not the trainer. You're training the trainer and granting him or her access to your proprietary knowledge, so that they can coach, educate, or consult with others.

Of course, there's a fee for others to license your intellectual property. This revenue opportunity is also fitting for people that want to scale this type of work and increase the revenue potential, without jeopardizing the quality of their content or the amount of time spent working.

5. Monetizing A Following

You've probably heard the term "advertising revenue model" mentioned before. For example, building an ad revenue model means you'll grow an audience large enough that other entities will want to pay you to be able to market their services or wares to your audience.

This revenue opportunity applies to authorities like you in the form of a podcast series, online community, or video series you might build. If you have a large group of listeners, readers, or watchers, then advertisers will likely want the opportunity to pay you to sponsor their activities and market their stuff to your community.

This revenue strategy requires building a large community, and therefore, the activities and work involved in this need to be seriously considered. Creating a new podcast each week, nurturing a community with probing questions, or creating a YouTube channel with tons of videos requires significant work, dedication, and time.

But, if building these audiences through the types of vehicles mentioned above interests you, monetizing the audience by selling advertising is a revenue stream you should consider.

6. Scoring More Clients Because Of Your Thought-Leadership Status

Earning more money from your core business (i.e. selling more of your primary products or services for higher prices and fees with less resistance and competition) is the primary reason for building an organization's authority in the market.

Often, the money earned from other revenue streams, such as books, potential keynotes, or workshops is inconsequential income compared to the primary offering of the organization. And in most cases, for all intents and purposes, these other forms of income become marketing line items that just so happen to earn revenue rather than cost money as an expense.

When your audience sees you as a thought leader, they're more apt to choose you versus a competitor. In many cases, your audience won't even bother entertaining competitive proposals or bids because you've established yourself as *the go-to person*, and working with you is seen as working with the best.

How To Identify Your Sources Of Revenue

Perhaps you've read these revenue stream examples, and you're wondering how to figure out what's best for you. Or perhaps you think all of the revenue streams are a good fit, but you're feeling overwhelmed and want to narrow down the list on where to start.

In either case, I suggest two activities that will surely help you.

First, study other thought leaders in other industries. Visit their websites and pay particular attention to how they get paid. What are they promoting that they get paid for? How adaptable are those things to your authority platform?

If all of this information is hidden, you might have to inquire by completing a form on their websites or by calling their phone numbers and playing the role of secret shopper. Tell them you are interested in their businesses and want to learn how you can hire them to help you. See how they describe their offerings and take notes that you can reference after you hang up the phone.

The second activity is to think about your audience persona and what would help your audience the most. In other words, think about what your audience would be eager to buy from you.

If you're unsure, look at your audience persona and identify some people that you know or could become connected with that are a match for that persona. Interview these "persona stand-ins," and tell them what you're thinking about selling. Ask them if they've ever wished there was something like your offering that they could buy.

If they say 'no,' ask them if they think people similar to them might buy something like that.

If they still say 'no,' ask them if they've ever wished they could purchase something to help them with stuff related to your authority topic. If they say 'yes,' ask them to describe what that offering might look like to them.

The intelligence you gain from these conversations will help you begin selecting the ways in which you'll earn money from your authority platform.

Once you begin getting clear on how you'll earn more revenue from your new authority platform, you'll need to build the website to capture leads and generate revenue. In the next chapter, we'll look at several key tactics you can implement immediately on your website to move visitors to action.

Chapter 6

Step 4: Build Your Online Presence

I n today's technology-driven, social-media-sharing world, every authority needs an online presence. Period. That's why, in this chapter, we'll explore what your online presence should look like and how you can build your authority platform online.

First, we'll tackle how you establish your presence online, whether that presence be your very own website or by adding content to your organization's website. Then, we'll discuss the critical things that need to be on your homepage and additional pages, how to make sure people can easily contact you, and lastly, the team of people you'll need to seek out to help you build this important online tool.

Determine Where Your Online Presence Should Be

If you dream of speaking, writing your own book, or earning revenue from your authority platform in any of the ways described in the last chapter, your website is the keystone of your online presence and a huge asset in helping you appear legitimate. In fact, when done right, your website can quickly decrease skepticism people may have about you and increase their confidence in you. Since you have an entrepreneurial vision for your authority platform, your website will be essential to successfully achieving that vision.

If you're an employer that's looking to grow your company's authority by leveraging your associates' and employees' activities, making thoughtful adjustments to your organization's existing website achieves the goal of creating a strong impression. When your company's website includes all the events your employees are speaking at, the events you're hosting yourselves, new blog topics, and downloadable ma-

LinkedIn for Intrapreneurs

If you're an intrapreneur and your authority will benefit the organization you're currently working for (or any future organizations you may join), your LinkedIn profile is the most beneficial place for you to brand your authority. That social platform is where your audience will connect with you, where they'll go to read your content, and where those future employers (and headhunters) will likely find you. If you happen to have an entrepreneurial vision for your authority that you'll independently earn money from in the future, I recommend you continue reading on.

terials, such as whitepapers and e-books, your company's Authority Multiplier becomes fully represented online.

At the end of this chapter, we'll discuss hiring a website designer, a copywriter, and a website developer to help you build or expand your website.

On the surface, you may be tempted to think they can run with the project while you focus on other things. However, without approaching your website with a thorough understanding of what makes a strong authority marketing website, you might come up short.

Even if you hire the most talented experts, you must strategically lead this project and ensure your website contains exactly what it needs to build your authority.

So, what does your website need? First, you must...

Create A Strong Impression on Your Homepage

Your homepage is the first, and perhaps only, impression you'll make on a prospective customer. People will either be intrigued to read more and continue looking at your website, or they won't. Without a compelling homepage that turns a browser into a reader, the rest of your website may as well not even exist. So, from an authority-marketing standpoint, crafting a homepage that grabs a visitor's attention and pulls him or her in is critical. Consider these key elements for your website's homepage:

Write a Compelling Headline

The headline of your website should be crafted to immediately establish your authority and describe the people you serve. Avoid industry jargon and unclear language. Instead, write a headline that clearly communicates that you're a leader in your niche.

For example, I could have a vague headline on my homepage that states, "Authority Marketing Services."

However, people visiting that website for the first time might wonder what that headline means and whether I work with people like them.

Instead, if I wrote a headline that explicitly stated that I'm "Helping Entrepreneurs, Speakers, and Authors Build Authority & Influence," you might understand more clearly a) the people I'm looking to serve, and b) the outcome of the services I offer.

When you're working on your own headline, make sure it communicates at least two of the following three critical elements:

1. The people you're looking to serve

2. The services or products you offer

3. The outcomes of your services or products

Choose Your Images Carefully

If you're an entrepreneur, your website should contain images of you in action. If you consult, your website should include photography of you working with your clients. If you speak and are looking for more speaking engagements, be sure to use images of you in the type of speaking environment you desire most, as well as a video of you speaking.

This means you'll need to seek out a professional photographer to capture images of you for your website. To make the process easier, I like to pull together ideas on a Pinterest board and share the board with a photographer. This little trick allows me to explain the images and visuals I'm looking for without wasting time or confusing the matter. The Pinterest board helps paint a clear picture of what I'm seeking and eliminates a photographer's need to guess.

If you're a larger organization, stock photography is acceptable. However, custom photography is still recommended as a stronger way to establish your authority. For an example of an entrepreneur that does a terrific job at establishing his authority utilizing photography and video, visit www.storybrand.com.

Include Your Revenue Sources (i.e., Your Products and Services)

Although your homepage's number one objective is establishing your authority, be sure to make hiring you or buying from you easy for people as well. Your homepage should highlight the service areas or product categories you're selling to your audience. Include small descriptions of each utilizing compelling copy that helps a visitor realize that you understand their needs and have a service or product to match. If you've written a book (or a few books), make sure there is an area of your homepage highlighting this "product" too.

Not showing your products and services on your home page and burying them elsewhere on your website limits people's ability to buy from you.

Include Your Authority Marketing Elements

Do you or your team members write a blog that helps to establish your authority? If so, include a blog feed highlighting three or four of your most recent posts. Are you routinely hosting events? Include high-level information on those events with links to learn more. Do you host a podcast? Include your three most popular episodes with a link to all the episodes.

Make It Easy to Connect on Social Media

Ensure that finding you on social media is easy for your customers by including your social media icons and links at either the top or bottom of your homepage. If you have not established social media profiles yet, I recommend starting with no more than three. Think about where your audience will likely connect with you and spend the most time and effort on those social platforms only. Otherwise, you run the risk of spreading your efforts too thin.

Offer Something for Free

When you offer something for free on your website, you can turn a website visitor into a lead or connection you can then nurture with ongoing email marketing campaigns. Not having a mechanism like this to generate a lead and build a relationship is a missed opportunity, because most website visitors leave without ever returning.

However, if you offer something for free in exchange for a visitor's email address, you're automatically building your prospect database. You're getting your website to do some sales work for you!

Here are some simple ideas for free things you can offer on your website:

- a free chapter of your book

- a whitepaper

- an informative video

- a tip sheet

- a calculator or assessment

- access to a research study or survey results

When you set up your freebie, be sure to connect your contact or sign-up form to your email marketing tool or customer relationship management (CRM) tool.

An all-in-one marketing tool I love is Hubspot. It provides exceptional marketing information and offers email marketing, as well as a CRM.

SharpSpring is another great all-in-one marketing tool and CRM system that is more cost-effective if you have a large email list.

For a third, less costly solution, consider Mail-Chimp. While not as sophisticated and although it's not a CRM, MailChimp offers a lower cost email marketing service with decent capabilities for those just starting out.

Outline Your Website's Navigation Menu

Now that you know how to grab a visitor's attention with your home page, plan out the rest of your site's navigation menu. There are seven pages you may want to consider creating or adding to your website:

1. About Me

2. Services or Products

3. Speaking

4. Books

5. Blog, Podcast, or Video Series

6. Events

7. Contact & Media Kit

About Me

Your "About" page should house your bio along with all the proof points from your body of work. Your bio should be written in the first person and include as much of your own personality as possible. I encourage you to make your bio interesting and inviting to read. After all, no one remembers a boring bio! For an example of an about page with loads of personality, visit www.kirahug.com/about. In the case of an organization's "About Us" page, I recommend having a summary of the organization followed by team biographies written in the third person.

Services or Products

Many authorities and organizations make their services and products page confusing. Don't do that! Resist the urge to use industry jargon or what I call "fluffy marketing language." Instead, be crystal clear with your visitors and make sure they know exactly what you are offering. For an example of a creative services page that clearly outlines the way services help a visitor resolve his or her issues, visit www.lrsuccess.com/needs-served.

Speaking

If you're looking to get paid to speak or invited to speak at industry events, make sure you have a page on your website that outlines the talks you deliver. When event planners visit this page, they should easily see the speeches you offer and be able to select one that's best for their events.

Be sure to include a form on your speaking page for event coordinators to use. This contact form doesn't have to be long or complex. Shorter forms have been proven to deliver higher conversion rates than longer forms. For a speaking form, I recommend asking the event planner's first name, last name, email address, phone number, and offering an optional text field where he or she can describe the event.

Consider including your own email address and phone number on this page, as well, so event planners can connect with you and discuss their upcoming conferences or events! For an example of an excellent speaker's page, visit www.ryanavery.com/keynotes.

Books

Whether you've written one book or many books, show off your efforts by displaying your books proudly. Include links to Amazon or wherever your books are sold. Highlight book reviews. This page is an instant authority-builder. Even if no one ever buys a book or reads one that you've written, just having them on your website boosts your credibility. For an example of an inspiring book page, visit www.brenebrown.com/books-audio.

Blog, Podcast, or Videos

Your authority platform will be reliant on the continuous content you publish, and your blog, vlog, or podcast pages are an essential part of establishing your thought leadership and building your authority. The method you choose should be whatever is easy, comfortable, and most importantly, a medium you can do consistently. We'll be covering this in much greater detail in the next chapter.

For now, no matter which method you choose, I encourage you to share those content pieces on your website whenever you release new material. For an example of an authority who shares her podcast on her blog every time a new one releases, visit www.clairepells.com/blog.

Events

If you host or attend events, make sure there is a page on your website that lists both upcoming and past events. The past events are important for building your authority and demonstrating the level of activity you've managed to create for your business. The future events are vital to attracting people to you. Therefore, be sure to include both! For an example of an "Events" page, visit www.foxrothschild.com/events.

Contact & Media Kit

This page is how you want people to contact you if they're interested in interviewing you, hiring you, or buying from you. Your "Contact" page is the most critical page of your website after your homepage. Resist the urge to just slap up a contact form. Be more thoughtful about the various ways you want your audience to connect with you. If you reach out to the media for press opportunities, be sure to have a media kit with approved biographies, images, and titles on this page. For an example, visit www.matthewsnewman.com/media-kit.

Similarly, if you're more interested in getting leads for sales opportunities from your website, make sure your contact page makes people feel comfortable to connect with you. And most importantly, set your potential clients' expectations for what'll come next after they reach out. For an example, visit www.11outof11.com/contact-us.

Hiring Talent To Design, Write, And Build Your Website

I want to close this chapter by encouraging you to invest in your website by hiring talented experts in website design, copywriting, and website development. There is a vast array of talent out there for each aspect that goes into a new website. So, to make the process easier, I suggest seeking out individuals that specialize in the areas that are important for authority websites.

In the case of website design, you want to find a designer that has experience with personal brands and designing a website for a thought leader. Also make sure the designer you select is experienced in responsive design, meaning that the website will stretch or shrink to various sizes depending on screen size, tablet, or mobile viewing.

For copywriting, seek out a conversion copywriter with experience in personal branding websites. He or she will help you establish your voice and tone online, as well as write the copy that'll convert a website visitor into a business opportunity or sale.

Lastly, your website developer should be working on a platform that's accessible by you and easily updateable. Consider a Wordpress or Hubspot developer so that you're able to easily add blog posts, new events, or update the information on your website in the future with ease.

Now you should have a clearer picture of what should be on your website and how to hire the right talent to create it for you. In the next chapter, we'll explore how you can establish a systematic approach to creating your content on an ongoing basis without falling behind or dragging your feet.

Chapter 7
Step 5: Create Thought-Leadership Content

When you constantly produce new content, you make following you easy for people. That's because you're able to release new ideas, contribute new commentary, and reward the people that want to pay attention to you. As a result, you stay top of mind and, unlike your blender competitors, you are not easily forgotten.

However, the sticking point for most people is the fact that creating content is challenging and time-consuming. After all, client work, family activities, and a million other items are constantly hitting your to-do list. Because of this feeling of overwhelm, most people never even start. Or, maybe they start but quickly get distracted and stop after a tiny burst of activity.

In this chapter, we'll cover how to create and build your content – what I call your "thought-leadership repository" – on an ongoing basis without falling behind, dragging your feet, or stopping. I'm a big believer in sticking with routines. We'll discuss how to establish a steady rhythm of content that'll grow your following and exposure in a way that's easy for you. You'll build a routine that doesn't take up too much of your time.

By the end of this chapter, you'll be itching to create new content for the world to see.

The Role Of Content Director

If you're an individual professional, the content creation process falls solely on your shoulders. You'll be in charge of the entire process, from planning your editorial topics, creating your content, reviewing your work, and publishing everything yourself. As you can imagine, this process is a lot of work for one person to handle. The role of Content Director will be added as one of the many hats you wear.

If you're an employer, on the other hand, you'll rely on your team's ability to contribute to the company's content creation efforts. Your team has a built-in advantage over the solo professional, since your organization has more resources and more potential authors of content for the company.

The biggest challenge for an organization with a team, however, is delegation and accountability. Yes, as an organization, your content creation effort can be spread out over your team, enabling each individual to assume a small amount of responsibility. But unless you have someone at the helm, delegating the workload and keeping the team accountable, you'll struggle to systematically create your thought-leadership repository.

To solve this issue, I recommend assigning the role of Content Director to an employee or an outsourced agency. If no one owns this role, content creation will fall by the wayside when client work gets in the way. And client work will get in the way!

Whether content creation is led by you, someone on your team, or an agency you outsource this work to, this responsibility is all about corralling the content and ensuring it's published routinely. In essence, the Content Director owns the content creation process from end to end, just like the editor of a magazine or newspaper.

Selecting Your Primary Form of Content

For most professionals, content comes in three primary types: written content, audio content, and video content. The simplest way to determine the type of content you'll produce is to decide what's easiest for you. This is imperative because you'll find continuously creating new content difficult if the format you choose is challenging for you. Avoid venturing down a path that you'll likely abort later because of difficulty or lack of comfort. Instead, choose the easiest path from the outset!

For example, if you or your employees hate being on camera, how will you produce a whole library of videos? You won't. Likewise, if you'd rather do just about anything other than write, how will you routinely write lengthy blog posts? Again, you won't. Distractions will occur. Client work will become more demanding. Opportunities will grow and begin to cannibalize your time.

As you're reading through this list of possible formats, consider what sounds most easy and comfortable to you:

- Writing blog posts

- Writing emails with your full content within each email

- Recording podcast episodes

- Recording videos on YouTube

- Recording Facebook Lives

- Recording Instagram Lives

- Creating webinars (either live or pre-recorded)

- Facilitating online groups, such as Facebook Groups or LinkedIn Groups

- Running live events, such as workshops or keynotes

If you're going to create new content with ease, remain committed to the process. If you're going to succeed at positioning yourself or your company as a thought leader in your industry, then you must choose the easiest format(s) to get started.

Including Outsiders (Or Not)

Some content creators include people outside their organizations on a regular basis. You see this with podcasts quite often. Even though the podcast is hosted by an individual entrepreneur or organization, each episode includes an interview with someone outside the hosting business. On the flip side, some podcasts are just an individual talking without any interviews.

Deciding whether or not you'll include outsiders should be something you think about in the beginning of your podcasting process. Then, continue to think about outsider interviews every so often as you continue to produce your content. Outsiders can be helpful contributors to offload creating all the content yourself. Interviewing a related thought leader or partner on a podcast results in less of a burden on you to plan all the talking points. Instead, you just have to come up with a few interview questions.

But also, note that when working with outsiders, you have to coordinate schedules and ensure your outsiders are meeting your standards for quality content. In the end, the actual time spent on the content is likely the same regardless of whether you or your employees do all the creation or if you invite outsiders to participate. The time is just spent doing different things within each model, such as outlining talking points if it's just you versus schedule coordination if it's you and someone you're interviewing.

Creating Your Thought-Leadership Angle

People often wonder what to write about, what to create a podcast series on, or what kinds of videos to shoot. The best thought leaders don't just wing it. Content strategy should be carefully planned, including what content topics you will cover as well as what you won't.

To get started, a simple approach is to create content that covers the same things you talk about with prospects and clients. Chances are, if your prospects and clients are interested, your followers will be too! These topics might include:

1. Top five tips you talk about with prospects

2. Commentary on other articles written

3. Things most clients don't know that they should

4. Misconceptions about your industry or niche

5. How some companies do things within your industry and how things can be done better

6. Client case studies

In addition to creating basic content, you must also create your content with a unique angle. For example, let's say your authority platform stars you as the expert at planning magical Disney World vacations for families with

young children. Your unique, authority platform is rooted in your belief that most Disney
World vacations are fun, but only if you know
how to limit your time in the parks.

Most content creators in your niche are writing about topics such as the best weeks to
travel to Disney, the best ways to beat Disney
lines, and the cheapest airlines flying in and
out of Orlando. The point of the other vacation
planners' blogs is to help families spend the
most time at the parks as possible.

You, on the other hand, hold the position that
the parks are overwhelming to young families.
They're hot, they're crowded, and they're usually the cause of skipped naps. And when you
surveyed a few children that recently went to
Disney, you learned that the park was not the
happiest place on earth for most of these kids.
You feel most park-goers overdo it and don't
understand the proper mix of park time and
relaxation, especially with young kids in tow.

Because your perspective is unique, your content will be different. You won't write about the topics mentioned by the other vacation planners. Instead, your content might cover things like how to ensure your child fondly remembers her Disney vacation, how to balance quiet time while at Disney, and how to ensure your child gets the rest he or she needs while traveling.

And because you're writing about what you truly believe, you're inspired to do more and more research on the topic of how parents make a Disney vacation enjoyable versus how some Disney-goers inadvertently make their vacations stressful.

Do you see how the angle's uniqueness creates more powerful and interesting content? When creating your content, remember that real, authority content doesn't cover the same thing your competitors cover. To be true thought-leadership content, you must create content that includes your unique perspective.

This is an extremely important concept, so we'll cover this in more depth in Chapter Nine.

Establishing a Rhythm of Content Creation

You might be wondering, "How often should I produce new content?" The right answer to

---

To Sell or Not to Sell?

I'm always asked the question, "Should I sell or not sell my stuff in my content?" Personally, I believe that there may be opportunities in your content to mention products or offerings. But mention your products subtly. No one looks forward to listening to, reading, or watching ads. So, if you want to establish a following as an authority and thought leader, I believe your content must to be 99% informative and educational, and only 1% sales.

this question comes in two forms: what's right for you and what's right for your audience.

I work with a number of clients that cannot imagine producing new content more than once a week. They choose to create content weekly not because they cannot keep up with a faster pace, but because their audiences cannot consume content any quicker.

For other clients, their packed schedules don't allow for fast content creation. They simply cannot produce new content more than once a week, even though their audience is hungry for more.

As you're planning out your content creation system, consider a realistic rhythm for both your audience and for you. The biggest secret for achieving this rhythm is working in advance of when content is needed and scheduling your content to be released on a later date.

In doing this, you'll be able to commit to a rhythm and stick to it. This rhythm is critical to keep your followers engaged because if you publish new content every two weeks, and then "disappear" for a few months because you've gotten busy, you'll lose all the momentum. In other words, you'll watch your thought-leader status that you worked so hard to build slip through your fingers. Not only that, you might lose followers too.

When you commit to creating content, commit to a schedule and rhythm.

Making Content Creation Systematic

Once you know who will act as your firm's Content Director, you have some ideas about the form your content will take, and you have ideas about your thought-leadership angle, it's time to start planning and creating. A successful Content Director creates a system from the start. Doing so will allow you to create content while running the rest of your business without anything falling through the cracks.

To get started, I recommend creating an editorial topic plan that includes a brain dump of topic ideas. My own editorial topic plan includes ideas that I want to cover at some time or another. Sometimes I plan out exact dates for topics being released. Other times, I just refer to my list of topics and pick one that I feel like working on.

When I'm planning exact release dates, it's usually because something time-sensitive is happening in my business. Perhaps I'm speaking at an event or planning to go to a conference. If the content's topic is related, then the timing for this particular piece of content is important. When content isn't quite as purposeful, I'll just pick from the ongoing list. Having that ongoing list is a big help, because having a plan ahead of time avoids a hiccup in content creation due to a lack of ideas. Just refer to the list and you're sure to find one that you fancy working on!

When scheduling the creation of new content, I sometimes get so inspired to work on a single topic that I work on the piece and knock out one, great, in-depth piece of content quickly.

However, the majority of the time, I block off two to three hours for content creation every month and create multiple pieces of content at once. Doing so allows me to have a repository of content ready to be scheduled for release so that I can take much-needed breaks from creating content. I often find that the breaks also give me time to think of new ideas, a practice which is great for adding to the ongoing list inside my editorial topic plan!

Plus, working on multiple pieces of content together is friendlier to my schedule. I simply schedule my few hours and head to a nearby coffee shop or lock myself away in my office.

In the next chapter, we'll discuss how to get the most out of your content and how to attract a following. In addition, we'll look at how to get the press and the media to pay attention, as well as how to get your name out to more people and build awareness.

Need More Help?

Need more help getting started and keeping your content organized? Don't worry. I've got you covered!

To help you create a system for creating your content, I've prepared an editorial topic-planning template for you.

The template enables you to uncover areas you might want to further study. The template also includes a spreadsheet for capturing your ideas, noting deadlines, and selecting the date on which you'll share each piece of content with the world.

To download the free, editorial topic-planning template, go to:

www.Angela-Pointon.com/stop-blending

Chapter 8

Step 6: Get Yourself Out There

E very time you publish something new, it's like shouting, "Is anyone out there?!" from the bottom of a canyon. You may feel like no one is reading, listening, or watching. But that's how every thought leader starts. Unfortunately, that's one of the reasons why so many quit too.

I recently took solace in looking waaaaay far back in Seth Godin's blog archives. His early posts might have gotten twenty likes or less. Some had no likes at all! Those early posts were a far cry from the 5,000 or more likes he gets every day from each of his current daily (yes, daily!) posts. It's important to note that Seth began blogging in 2002. What's even more important to note is that he didn't give up!

If you're going to establish yourself as an authority, then you've got to start somewhere. And the sooner you start, the sooner you'll grow your thought-leadership following – as long as you don't quit. Yes, your following will most likely grow slowly at first. But as more people learn about the content you're sharing, more people will share your content with others and so on.

That said, there are a few key tactics you can implement to escalate the speed at which you leave ground zero and grow the amount of people that get your content and create a bigger impression. We'll cover each of these tactics in this chapter.

Always Share Your Content

Whenever you create a new piece of content, be sure to share your efforts in a number of ways. For example, the first way to share your content is to email your content to your company's database. Your database should consist of customers, prospects, partners, and referral sources. Depending on how often you're publishing content, be sure to share your content via email every time you publish or once a month at a minimum.

Whenever I'm sharing a piece of content with my audience, I write a short lead-in paragraph or two that gives my audience a highlight of what's covered in the content. Then, I include a hyperlink and a button at the end of the email that leads them to the piece of content.

The reason I write the email this way, rather than including a lot of the content in the email, is because I want to get my people to my website so that they have the ability to explore other pages while they're there. Plus, structuring the email to encourage readers to click also allows me to measure how many people go from my emails to my website. Without these stats, I wouldn't be able to see which topics are most popular and which topics are least popular.

The second way to share your content is via your own social media. Your content should be shared on your company's social media accounts as well as your own personal accounts. Social media sharing is free, and the more reach you can create, the better.

To improve the number of people re-sharing your content, ask a few referral sources or partners to be part of your social sharing initiative. Offer to occasionally share their content if they'll occasionally share yours. And whenever you produce a new piece of content that you feel suits their audiences, be sure to send off a quick email kindly nudging them to share the new content. As a best practice, always ask what you can do to help them inside the same email!

Before we move on, I want to offer a word of caution. When you're new to creating content, sharing your content with others can be scary. Some people I've talked to get worried that their competitors will steal their content, especially clients that are just starting out. Because of this, they think not sharing the content is safer. This couldn't be further from the truth. Ask yourself this question, "Which is the primary master you're serving here?" Being seen as a thought leader by your audience or fearing your competition? The answer is obvious, so share your content and position yourself as the authority you are.

Getting Even More Visibility

The premier way to get even more visibility on your content is to pitch your content to other sources. Earlier in this book, I mentioned that I used to be an authority on marketing for photographers. I truly started at ground zero. I threw together my first website, set up social media profiles, and set up an account with a popular email marketing tool. But I had no followers and no contacts on my email list.

Still, I blogged every week and consistently published new content. I tried following people on Twitter, and a few people even followed me back. This was an exciting and encouraging beginning! I posted every blog entry on social media. Before long, I got a direct message from a Twitter follower that also gave business advice to photographers. We set up a conference call, and we "clicked" right away. By the end of the call, we decided we wanted to co-host a webinar with some of the photography industry's top photographers.

Co-hosting a webinar was a lofty goal, but we decided to go for it. In exchange for me doing all the grunt work of organizing the webinar and inviting all the speakers, he agreed to promote the webinar to his list of roughly 3,000 people.

The webinar was a hit! We had over 200 people registered, and we managed to attract some great speakers who were all willing to present during the webinar for free. At the end of the webinar, those 200 people became the first people on my email list. My email list grew month after month from there.

Before long, I received another direct message on Twitter. This time, the message was from an editor of a national photography association's monthly magazine. The writer of the magazine's marketing column recently left to take another job, and the editor offered me the spot! The position was unpaid, but it was so in line with my audience and my authority platform that I said, "Yes!" in mere seconds.

I had no idea what would come of this kind of exposure. Every time an issue came out, I added new social media followers and more people asked to join my email list. Over time, I secured clients from the column as well. Recently, someone emailed me and told me he was going through old clippings of the magazine and wanted to hire me as a coach, even though I stopped writing the column a few years ago.

Needless to say, partnering with others and getting exposure to a larger audience is a great way to quickly escalate your authority as well as increase both your and your partners' social media followings and email databases.

How To Pitch Your Content

"Pitching" is the word used to describe cold calling or emailing someone to start up a conversation about getting coverage or being featured. In a big company, pitching content is typically the job of a publicist or public relations department.

For content creators, pitching can be a great way to leverage someone else's audience and get more exposure. However, when you pitch your content, you must pay careful attention to how you pitch.

To help you understand how to pitch, I suggest following these three rules:

1. Know Their Content

Blindly pitching without taking the time to know the other person's content is the fastest way to get your email deleted or get your direct message ignored. You don't have to be a constant listener or reader to pitch, but you do have to do a little homework. Read, listen to, or watch a few pieces of content this other person has created – especially topics you find interesting. Make a few notes of interesting tidbits or things you especially liked.

2. Make Your Pitch About Them, First

When you're emailing or direct messaging another content creator, whether you want the other person to participate in a blog, podcast, magazine, webinar series, or something else entirely, your message needs to be 90% about him or her.

Start your outreach by mentioning the things you loved most about the content you researched in the point above. "I just wanted to reach out to you because I really loved your recent piece on XYZ," is a great way to begin your pitch. Go on to be specific, proving that you really did take your time researching him or her.

Then, in the close of the email, describe yourself. Writing, "I am a thought leader in my industry on ABC and would love to chat with you sometime, if you're ever interested," is a great way to conclude the email. Be sure to include your contact information and your website address. If you have a particular topic in mind that you feel would be great for their audience, don't hesitate to mention the topic as well.

Again, however you close out your pitch, the parts about you and your content should only be 10% of what you write. The majority should be commenting on particular things you liked about the person's content.

3. Aim High

I never thought I'd be a columnist for a national magazine hitting hundreds of thousands of my target customers. This is why I encourage you to aim high. As you draft up a list of potential outlets to pitch, include some that'll be easy wins – such as partners or people already familiar with you. But include some outlets that are a stretch too.

My rule of thumb when pitching is to try to get one hundred 'no's.' If you're shooting for that many no's, you're bound to get a few yeses along the way too!

You May Still Have to Write It

The editorial staff of magazines, newspapers, and content-based websites is shrinking due to a lack of paid advertising that once supported a much larger staff. As a result, if you want your content published, you may end up writing your own editorials on behalf of the publication to which you're pitching. I've always looked at this as a good thing! I get to control the content in the piece. Even though the editorial staff will review the content and may advise edits, at least the editorial is starting out in the best state for your potential clients from the get-go.

The Paid Speaking World

The last venue for additional exposure that I'll cover is paid speaking.

Paid speaking opportunities may naturally come as a result of your growing exposure. They did for me. After I secured the spot as the columnist in the photography association's magazine for the United States, the Canadian counterpart invited me to their annual convention as their keynote speaker. That keynote was a paid speaking opportunity, including paid lodging and air travel.

But breaking into the paid speaking world doesn't have to happen this way. For many people, getting paid speaking opportunities happens after pitching smaller conferences and events or after doing a few speaking gigs for free.

Research venues that might make good outlets for your content. Larger events will have calls for presentations, and you can submit your proposal to them for review. Other events won't openly advertise opportunities like this and will require you to research, contact, and pitch the event coordinators.

Remember, getting paid to speak isn't necessarily the *only* way to get in front of a live audience. Speaking for free in front of the right audience might get you just as much exposure as paid events do.

Chapter 9

Step 7: Go from Ordinary Professional to True Thought Leader

Remember my red hair story from Chapter One and how I realized that "blenders" cannot be thought leaders? In that story, you learned that if you're going to become an authority in your field, you have to embrace your uniqueness and stop trying to blend in.

In this final chapter, I want to discuss how you can take your own unique opinions, perspectives, and insights related to the work you do and become a true thought leader in your field.

Ordinary Professionals Blend In

Despite believing that they stand out, the majority of professionals and organizations today are ordinary. They're not unique in their products or services, in the way they market themselves, or in how they help their customers buy. In other words, most professionals and organizations today are blenders.

To give you a simple visual of what a blender looks like in the business world, imagine the nine squares on the next page represent you (in the middle) and your eight competitors.

All squares are equal in how they appear from the outside, and no one company sticks out.

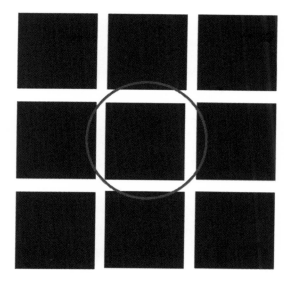

The biggest problem with a blender isn't that they know they're a blender and are damn proud of it. It's that they don't know they're blending in. And while the blender sees nuances that they believe are significant, the outside world doesn't notice those things at all. In reality, like the nine squares above, the outside world sees the blender and the competitors as identical companies, all looking the same. Similar companies. Similar offerings. All blending together.

For instance, take the bottled water industry. Not long ago, there were only a few varieties on store shelves. If you wanted a bottle of water back when you were a child, you selected from one or two brands. Today, go into any major grocery store, and you'll see an entire aisle dedicated to the most mundane beverage on the planet.

Not only that, the water companies now have mineral water, sparkling water, vitamin-infused water, purified water, artisan water, and the list goes on. In addition, each brand offers different shaped and sized bottles from which to select. The irony? Talk to the heads of marketing at any of the water brands, and they'll vehemently defend their product as being – you guessed it – different.

Here's problem with this mistaken perception about what makes something truly different. As Harvard Professor and marketing expert,

Young Me Moon, explains, the consumer can get confused with by selecting what's right for them when everything looks the same. The various products can lose their meaning and no longer stand out. Moon notes in her book, *Different*, that a variety of factors, from the explosion of information in the digital age to glutted markets of products, have led to a reduction in brand loyalty.

Moon's solution is for businesses to stop looking at differentiation as the "offspring of competition," and start seeing differentiation as "an escape from competition altogether." Achieving thought-leader status is the key to escaping your competition and transitioning from a blender to an industry authority.

So, how do you position yourself as an authority and escape the competition? There are two ways, and you'll notice that one way is much simpler than the other.

The first is to reach a point of true differentiation by offering a completely unique product or service. A company that offers products and services that are totally different than what's on the market today have the best opportunity to stand out and dominate the market.

Take Dollar Shave Club, for example. The idea of mail order razor blade replacements hadn't been tackled before they came along. Dollar Shave Club created a new, unique service within a product category full of blenders. Their concept of a mail order service was truly different.

Of course, timing is everything. There have been dozens and dozens of unique products and services that were ahead of their time but fell flat due to a lack of interest or understanding. If your timing is right and the market has been yearning for your unique product or service, you may experience explosive growth from the start.

However, the real issue is that **creating a truly differentiated product or service that people are yearning for is *hard***.

That's why your second option for becoming an authority is a more attainable approach for standing out from the crowd. So, what's the second option? To market your products, services, and ideas through content that positions you as the authority.

Creating Content to Position Yourself as an Authority

Historically, getting your message out to the world was done through big ad campaigns and billboards. Today, entrepreneurs and companies are positioning themselves as thought leaders by crafting relevant content and leveraging the power of content marketing to grow their audiences and businesses.

Like we've discussed throughout this book, when you educate your audience with relevant, quality content, you go from a blender to an authority in your audience's mind. And as you stand out from your competition, your competitive environment starts to look like this, with you being the white square in the middle:

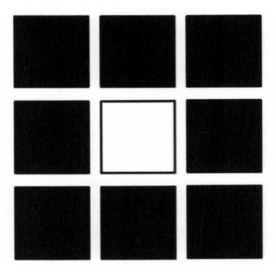

However, we don't live in a theoretical world. In reality, most of us have other competitors that are already using the same strategy and creating content to stand out. Or if your competition is smart, they'll eventually catch onto what you're doing and start creating content as well.

And before you know it, your ecosystem looks more like this, with a few blenders and a few unique ones—you included—starting to stand out:

Ten years ago, content creators were rare. Nowadays, oodles of individuals and organizations routinely create new content to position themselves as authorities. And as more of your competition chases the authority spotlight, the industry becomes noisier, and customers become inundated.

When this occurs, the true meaning of authority gets lost.

But that doesn't mean you shouldn't create content. In fact, creating relevant, quality content is the most practical and attainable approach to standing out from the crowd. You've simply got to up your game. And to do that, the content you create needs to be different.

Developing Your True Thought-Leadership Platform

Unlike you, most content creators do not understand their authority or thought-leadership platform. They haven't strategically thought about that all-important platform in the ways suggested in this book. They've yet to focus on how they, as thought leaders, see things differently. As a result, most content runs the risk of getting lost in the sea of information available today.

A true thought leader brings a higher level of thinking to his or her industry. They think strategically about the problems the industry faces. They notice dysfunction or opportunity and suggest another way to think about things or another way to do something. And rather than creating ho-hum content that any content creator can spew out, a true thought leader expresses his or her ideas in a new, unique way and gives the audience a new perspective.

In fact, contrary to what many people think, authority isn't created because of the breadth of reach. I believe the authorities that build a true thought-leadership platform earn respect more so because of the depth of their ideas and the perspective they offer.

Take some of the entrepreneurial world's most well-known authority content creators, for example. Individuals like Seth Godin, Gary Vaynerchuk, and Susan Cain do not shy away from sharing their viewpoint and how they believe things should be done in business. They don't talk about the same things, and they don't create content that's just like everyone else's content.

Seth takes a unique view on marketing, notices how poorly people market, and the common mistakes people make when advertising their products or services. And he writes about these mistakes every day on his blog.

Gary Vee, as people refer to him, believes strongly in entrepreneurship and that seizing opportunities quickly is critical to success. He routinely creates new video content to help people embrace the opportunities in front of them.

Susan has built a tribe of introverts by creating her "Quiet Revolution," a website with content aimed at recognizing the advantages of introverts in the workforce.

By mimicking the behaviors of Seth, Gary, and Susan, you will no longer stop at simply noticing a better way to approach things. You'll notice these better approaches, study them, try little experiments, and then share your thoughts, strategies, and findings with the world.

Developing Perspectives Like A True Thought Leader

Thought leaders and authorities are chronically curious. Despite how obvious this may seem, without fierce fascination about studying a topic, you'll quickly grow bored of your study. If you aim to be a true thought leader, the perspective you're curious about should also be something you're wildly passionate about.

As you explore your own curiosity, you'll notice your ideas and perspectives can become infectious. Your spouse or friends might roll their eyes and grow tired of your interest. But others that share those same interests will become eager to talk to you more. That's how thought leaders develop community, network, and leverage relationships made through their studies.

For some thought leaders, studying means a dedication to tests, exploration, assessments, and interviewing academics. For others, studying is the simple act of observing how people react to their methods, how their methods impact their businesses and the people around them, and the positive outcomes they achieve.

The depth of research and how much you study when forming your perspective is up to you, so long as you're sharing your work, thoughts, and insights via your content.

You should also be aware that some people may disagree with your perspective – either silently or out loud. That's okay. As you share your perspective and build your thought-leadership platform, if your perspective is strong, you'll have some haters. The people that share your passion and perspective matter much more than the haters.

Settling on a Tone

Every thought leader has a tone to his or her content, whether the content is written or spoken out loud. Someone's tone might be academic, light and humorous, or the tone might be no-nonsense. What's most important is letting your own tone shine through. Let's take a look at a few examples.

Suze Orman gives financial advice for real people delivered in her signature, no-nonsense tone. Orman is in a crowded market of financial advisors. But her straight-to-the-point commitment to the people that follow her distinguishes her from Dave Ramsey and other "competitors" in her space.

Abby Wambach is a two-time Olympic gold medalist, FIFA World Cup Champion, and the all-time highest international goal scorer for both male and female soccer players. In a word, she's tough. Her tone is tough too. In her retirement, she became an author and speaker. Inside a crowded environment of women's leadership and getting a voice at the table, Abby stands out as someone that lacks the soft, nurturing approach that so many others offer.

Jonathan Fields is a national bestselling author and the founder of *Good Life Project*®, one of the top-ranked podcasts in the world. Yet unlike most motivational coaches, he's not vibrant, loud, and stereotypically motivating in a rah-rah way. Listen to just a few minutes of any of Fields's podcasts, and you'll find he's quite the opposite. As he speaks in mere whispers and has a calming presence akin to a vocal massage, his tone is arguably the most unique in his field.

Plainly stated, your tone should match how you'd normally speak. However, note how your tone differs from your competition. Leverage that difference, emphasize your uniqueness, and take comfort that your individual tone can further set you apart.

How to Get Started

I encourage you to follow a few authority content creators that are of interest to you. Think of individuals that offer a unique perspective about something you're interested in. For me, I follow thought leaders in a range of topics such as photography, entrepreneurship, music, soccer, politics, social justice, feminism, and even food.

Whatever your extracurricular interests are, find a thought leader for a few interests and binge their content. Start listening, reading, or watching when these thought leaders release new stuff. Pay careful attention to their content and make note of the ways in which their perspectives and their tone are dissimilar to other content creators in their industry and niche.

Witnessing other thought leaders' successes will inevitably give you ideas and boost your confidence in publishing your unique thoughts and ideas. In addition, modeling authorities that stick out from the pack with their unique ideas, perspectives, and tone will help you think about breaking up the pattern within your own marketplace.

Like the diagram on the next page, a true thought leader's platform allows him or her to stand out, break the pattern that the other competitors follow, and gain attention because of their authority position.

By creating consistent content and putting your own unique spin and perspective on your content, you too can become a true thought leader to your audience and stand out from the crowd.

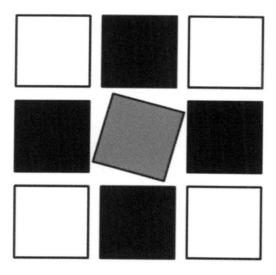

Your Next Steps

Congratulations for reading through all seven steps for achieving thought-leadership status. I'll reiterate one last time that as soon as you decide to become an authority on a topic, you've begun. And as you adopt the seven steps laid out in this book, you'll build upon that authority and achieve the thought-leadership status you crave and deserve.

But let's be honest here. Despite the teachings in this book, initiating the actual work recommended inside this book can be overwhelming and daunting. When you go to start your first blog post, you might stare at a blank cursor for twenty minutes. Or when you go to email a pitch to someone, you might spend ten minutes trying to locate an email address for him or her only to give up.

Believe me, I've been there myself.

And so to help you further along this path, I've created the exact online training program that I personally wished had existed to guide me through each step of my own journey and make things easier. I promise, the information is simple to digest!

The training is called ***Become A Thought Leader Practically Overnight*** and you can get access to it at:

www.Angela-Pointon.com/stop-blending

Inside this online training, you'll:

- Learn how to break down your body of work and leverage your real-life experience and expertise on your LinkedIn profile.

- See the exact process I use to help clients define their authority platform, including a behind-the-scenes look at how you can create your own authority-positioning website.

- Discover how to take advantage of the editorial topic-planning template I gifted you in Chapter Seven, so you can start creating content at will without any hesitation or anxiety.

- Get an exclusive sneak peek into my Pitch Outreach Program, and learn how you can make your pitches POP!

- And much more!

By leveraging this book and going through the online training, you'll be well on your way to achieving thought-leadership status. Soon, you'll enjoy the benefits of growing your revenue and widening your net via referrals, closing deals faster, and beating the competition.

-Angela Pointon

About the Author

From training, coaching, and leading her own content marketing agency called, 11outof11, Angela guides some of the world's most successful entrepreneurs on how they can stand out. She's a magazine columnist, frequent podcast guest, and a keynote speaker.

Angela can be found online at:
www.angela-pointon.com
www.11outof11.com

When Angela isn't working, she can be found spending time reading, writing, or petting her rescue dog, Bernie. Angela resides just outside Philadelphia, PA with her two sons and her husband.

Looking For An Engaging, Story-Telling Keynote Speaker?

Are you looking for someone who has the audience on the edge of their seats, raving about your event afterwards?

Do you need a keynote speaker that will not just inspire the audience but will leave them with key takeaways to implement immediately?

Are you seeking someone who has delivered talks, workshops, and keynote addresses to organizations and companies internationally?

If you answered "YES" to any of these questions, then Angela Pointon is the right speaker for you.

Angela has given dozens of speeches to business owners, association members, and entrepreneurs over the past decade - including traveling abroad to deliver keynote addresses on marketing and thought leadership.

She's shared stories, made audiences laugh, and given people real, actionable steps they can implement.

And she's provided marketing advice via a monthly magazine column that's delivered to over 100,000 people in the United States each month.

To Inquire About Having Angela Speak
At Your Event, Contact Her At This Email
Address:

hello@angela-pointon.com